MUMMY MONSTER
came to visit

Aly Walsh

Illustrations by Amanda Borchers

Mummy Monster

Copyright © Aly Walsh
Illustration copyright © Amanda Borchers

First Edition 2018
Published by Aly's Books

www.alysbooks.com
Your Book | Our Mission

Designed by Fish Biscuit
fishbiscuitdesign.com.au

All rights reserved. No part of this book may be reproduced or transmitted in any form or by any means, electronic, mechanical, photocopying or otherwise without the prior permission of the publisher.

ISBN: 9780664851112

Inspired by my daughter

Mummy Monster came to visit me today.

I don't know why – what did I do, or what did I say?

One minute Mum was fine and then the Mummy Monster appeared.

Where did she come from?

She's so mighty and she should be feared!

I can't work it out so let's go back to see.

Why did Mummy Monster make this visit to me?

On this one school day, Mum woke me with her usual beautiful smile.

She gave me five minutes to get up… easy, that's a very long while.

I could hear her suddenly calling my name.

But whoops, I am distracted practising for my next lacrosse game.

By the time she came stomping down the long hall, I had started brushing my hair…

But oh my goodness, when did she become so tall?

In the kitchen my breakfast greeted me.

Oh look it's my colouring-in book,
looking so neat and so pretty.

I colour so well, won't my Mum be happy.

Why all of a sudden is she sounding so angry?

I start getting dressed won't Mum be delighted!

My favourite song came on – high kicks, cartwheels and handstands I started.

Why is Mum now giving me a glare, doesn't she like my dancing hair?

Whoops, I look down and I am not dressed.

The race is nearly finished. I'd better do my best.

Mum will be excited because I am on my way.

Oh what's that… it's Madi our dog wanting to play.

Whoops what did I hear Mum just say?

I heard her yelling – was it at me or my brother?

Oh, now I'm distracted again, oh bother.

I don't know where she came from or when she appeared.

Where is my mummy, for Mummy Monster is now here?

Her clothes are all creased and she is now ten feet tall.

She is yelling in another language – or at least that is what I have been told.

Her hair is everywhere and her hands waving all around. She looks like a beast out of a story-book I found.

Was it me that made this Mummy Monster appear?

Please come back Mummy, make Mummy Monster disappear!

I promise tomorrow that I will do my best.

To eat my breakfast, brush my teeth, put my shoes on, make my bed and get dressed.

But sometimes it's hard for such a little one, to not be so distracted and find everything fun.

I love you my Mummy, please don't send the monster back.

Many kisses and hugs for you.

…ohhhhhh what's that?

www.ingramcontent.com/pod-product-compliance
Lightning Source LLC
Chambersburg PA
CBHW041429010526
44107CB00045B/1550